ELLA
Diaries
TOP SECRET!

For Tia and Inez:
flash storywriters and dancers!— M.C.

For Scarlett, Violet, Elsie, Dusty,
Meg and Dan.— D.M

Scholastic Australia
An imprint of Scholastic Australia Pty Limited
PO Box 579 Gosford NSW 2250
ABN 11 000 614 577
www.scholastic.com.au

Part of the Scholastic Group
Sydney • Auckland • New York • Toronto • London • Mexico City
New Delhi • Hong Kong • Buenos Aires • Puerto Rico

Published by Scholastic Australia in 2023.


ISBN: 978-93-5471-610-2

Typeset in Sweetie Pie.

NATIONAL LIBRARY OF AUSTRALIA A catalogue record for this book is available from the National Library of Australia

This edition 2024

This reprint edition April 2025

Printed in India at Shivam Offset Press, New Delhi

# ELLA Diaries

## Flash Mob Fever

**Saturday night, in bed**

Dear Diary,

It was an exCEPTionally sunnerous sunny day today.

So sunnerous, Mum and I decided to take Bob for a nice walk to the park.

At the park we saw little kids playing on the swings

and kicking soccer balls to each other

and dogs chasing each other around and around in circles (including Bob)

and pretty ducks swimming on the pond.

We also saw some big kids putting on a **circus show** for their family.

One of the kids was tightrope-walking along a rope tied between two trees.

Another one was **juggling** with juggling sticks,

tossing them **UP UP UP** into the air.

And another one was **clomping** around clomperously on **giganterous** stilts.

The other people in their family thought they were aMAZing. And Excellent. And **fanTABulously fabulous**.

And so did my mum. She had the **BIGGEREST** smile on her face the whole time she was watching them. As big as the smile on a **cute little quokka's face** when it also sees something it loves.

And she didn't stop smiling or talking about the clever circus kids the **WHOLE WAY HOME**.

I wish I could do something as clever as that. ☺

Good night, Diary.

Sweet dreams.

Love,

Ella

XOXO

## About ten minutes later . . .

I can't stop thinking about Mum's face while she was watching those kids doing the circus tricks.

She looked really, really, REALLY happy!

She's been SUPER busy lately, staying up really late working on importerant projects for her job.

And making time to cheer for us when we go in big races on sports days.

And doing lots of other parent-type stuff.

Maybe I could do something that makes her feel that happy too!

**But what, exactly?**

Hmmm . . .

Ella

XXX

## About ten minutes after that . . .

I've just had the most EXCELLENT (and also WONDERFUL and MARVELLOUS) idea!

It's going to be Mother's Day soon!

Olivia and Max and I always do something special for Mum on Mother's Day every year.

Like making her breakfast in bed.

Or baking and decorating a special cake.

Or giving her a fancy manicure and/or facial.

So this year, maybe I can do something **extra EXTRA special**, to show Mum how much I love and ~~apreesh~~ ~~apprech~~ appreciate her.

Except I STILL don't know what.

I need to go on a **SERIOUS SECRET MISSION** (SSM for short) to find out!

Hang in there, Diary. I'll be back soon!

Ella ♥

**8.3426 minutes later . . .**

I'm back!

Here's what happened on my SSM.

I carefully climbed out of bed and sneakily crept—**ninja-style**—down the hallway . . .

. . . past the lounge room where Mum and Dad were watching a funny show on TV . . .

. . . and up the **creakerous stairs** to Olivia's room, to see if she had any good ideas for a new, IMPROVED Mother's Day treat.

MY SSM
MY (empty) BED
DAD
MUM
ME
(CREEPING CREEPEROUSLY)
HahaHa HeHeHe!
CREAKEROUS STAIRS
OLIVIA
OLIVIA'S 'PRETEND' TIME MACHINE

which all turned out to be one big HORRENDOUSLY HOPELESS (and also TOTALLY TIME-WASTERING) mistake. ☹

That's because I found **THIS** taped to the outside of Olivia's bedroom door.

I was **SHOCKED!**

How did she even know I'd been thinking about the time machine thing? It's like she can read my mind or something.

Looks like I'm going to have to ask someone else in our family for help. But who?

## Twenty seconds later . . .

I know! Zoe and Ammy! They're not ~~acksh~~ actually in my family but they both know us all really well. And they ALWAYS have good ideas about stuff like this. (Mostly.)

Plus they also have mums. ☺

I'm going to call them FIRST THING tomorrow! ☺☺☺

E xxx

## Sunday, before dinner

Dear Diary,

I rang Zoe and Ammy **SECOND*** thing this morning.

* That is because **FIRST** thing this morning. Dad was making his **famous special pancakes** with maple syrup (plus optional blueberries and/or strawberries). And I didn't want my **greedy guts** little sister and brother to eat them all while I was on the phone.

AND ALSO **ANNOYING**

Zoe and Ammy both thought my idea of doing a Super Special Mother's Day Activity (SSMDA) this year was an excellent one. SO excellent that they both want to do an extra-special activity for their mums as well. Maybe even the SAME one I was going to do. ☺

So we had a **Super Special Mother's Day Activity Emergency Meeting** (SSMDAEM for short) about it this afternoon. We (mostly) always have them here in my bedroom. Except this time, I needed to find a new place.

That's because my **annoying little sister** Olivia (and also her BFF Matilda) has been even more annoying than usual lately. **EsPECially** if I have some of my friends over to do something special or importerant in my room.

Like working on a guest list for Zoe's birthday party.

Or planning our outfits for the school disco.

So this time we decided to have our SSMDAEM in Zoe's bedroom instead. HEHEHE. I cunningly sneaked out of the house (wearing my **besterest disguise**) while Olivia and Matilda were setting up their new IMPROVED spycam in the pear tree. ☺☺☺

Zoe doesn't need to worry about annoying little sisters and their BFFs spying on her when she's in her bedroom. That's because she only has an older brother, called Will. And he's usually too busy playing computer games or football with his mates to worry about what WE'RE doing. ☺

First of all, we ate all the snacks. Including an aMAZing chocolate meringue cake Zoe's nonna made.

Zoe said she should be the scribe* this time because she had some brand new glitter pens she wanted to try out.

* A scribe is the person in your group or on your special organisering committee who writes everything down.

Which was a teeny tiny bit unfair, Diary. Because she could see that I'd brought MY OWN special jumbo pack of glitter pens (and also notebook) all the way over to her place, in case I was the one elected to be the scribe.

In the end we had a nice friendly game of Rock, Paper, Scissors to help sort it out.

**Which Zoe won.** ☹

The next thing we di

Sorry, Diary. Dad just called me to say dinner was ready. I'll be back soon, pinky promise!

Ella

## About an hour later . . .

I'm back! We had schnitzels for dinner. And pineapple upside-down cake. Yum!

So anyway, after that we had a BIG importerant discussion about what activity we could do for our mums.

Here are our TOP FIVE ideas (and why or why not they would be good ones).

We needed a giganterous piece of paper to write ~~this~~ them all down.

| Activity Suggestions | Whose Idea |
|---|---|
| Circus tricks (like the ones the big kids did in the park). | Mine |
| Put on a ballet like Swan Lake. Or even one called Duck Lake (because there are lots of pretty ducks in the pond in our park). | Zoe's |
| Write and perform a musical. | Ammy's |

# Chance of Success

0%

Too hard to learn them all before Mother's Day.

40%

It might be too trickerous to find all the feathers for the costumes.

0%

Musicals are exTREMEly long. What if our mums got bored and went home early?

| | | |
|---|---|---|
| Make a video of our mums telling us their life story. With us asking them importerant questions like: 'Did you have many BFFs at school?'   | Mine | |
| Do a cheer squad thing like they have at some basketball and footy games. Except we would cheer on our mums.<br>Like this:<br>Give us an M!<br>Give us a U!<br>Give us an M - U - M spells<br>MUM! | Zoe's | |

55%

This one could be really good and also fun. Unless one of the mums had a very, very bad memory.

---

60%

Cheer squad people do lots of gymnastical moves (perfect for Zoe and me) and also shake streamers around a lot (which Ammy could do). But it would all be over VERY quickly.

Ammy and Zoe and I looked at each other with sadderous eyes. We'd written down the toppest of our top ideas and they were all hopelessly hopeless.

It was so not fair. Our mums deserve something excellent and aMAZing and fabulously fabulous. Not just another boring old breakfast in bed with burnt toast. Or a bunch of flowers from the garden. ☹

And then . . . all of a sudden . . . a brilliant idea FLASHED into my brain!! Just like a streak of streakerous lightning.

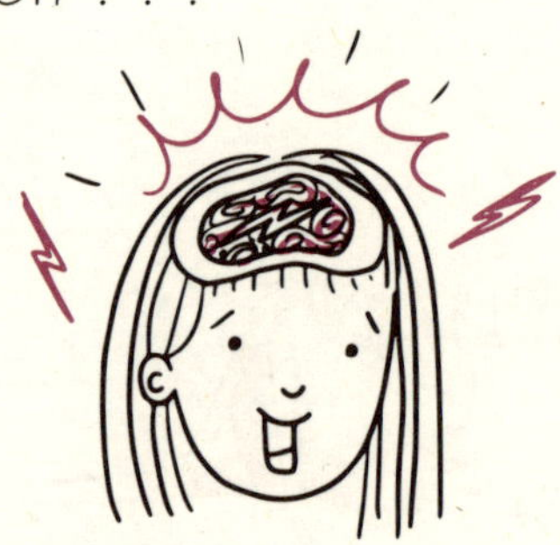

I started jumping up and down madly like a mad thing.

So then I gave them a big ~~explanashun~~ explanation all about how flash mobs work.

A flash mob is this **fantabulous** type of group dance that people do together. I saw one at our local shopping centre one day when I was out shopping for new shoes with Mum and Olivia.

It started out as one single lonely only person, standing all by themself like they were waiting for their BFF to turn up.

And then another person turned up, and started having a chat with them.

And then more and more people came out of nowhere until there were pazillions of them. And they were **ALL DANCING THE EXACT SAME DANCE**.

And it looked like this:

And there were other people doing drumming on African drums at the side, to make the music for them.

The dancers were stepping and jumping and swaying from side to side and waving their arms around in the air. And they were doing it all at ~~exackly~~ **exactly** the same time—just like synchronised swimmers do. ☺

And then the dance finished and . . . **POUFF!** The flash mobbers all went back to where they came from, just like that. It was like they hadn't ever even been there at all.

It was all so exciterating, Diary! And guess what? You can do **flash mobs** in all kinds of places! Like in food courts or city squares or even on trams or trains!

And then after I'd finished explaining everything, I had the most **brilliant** idea of all.

YES! A flash mob is PERFECT for our SSMDA.

I can't wait to get started on it!

Yours forever,
Ella
XXXX

## Monday, after school

Dear Diary,

Zoe and Ammy and I **couldn't stop talking** about our SSMDA at school today.

Before school

and at recess time

and waiting in the queue for the girls' toilets

and even while we were working on our projects! I don't think Ms Weiss was very happy about that though. ☹

But we did MOST of our talking at lunchtime.

Here are some of the things we chatted about (and wrote down in our special

SSMDA notebook) while we were talking.

**1** We need **MORE PEOPLE** in our flash mob than just the three of us.

**2a** We won't do tryouts this time, like we usually do when we're organisering a big event*. Which means we won't have to make any special posters** for it.

* Like a concert or a synchronised swimming demonstration for our school fundraiser.

** Which is a bit sadderous to the power of eleven, Diary, because I ♥ making posters. **EsPECially** ones where I get to use my Big Box of Craft Things to add special touches. ☹

**2b** Instead of having tryouts, we will just ask people we think will do a **good job** and not be all precious and show-ponyish about it.

**3** Names of people we could ask to join our flash mob:

- Poppy and Chloe and Daisy and Georgia (our **second-best friends**)

- Cordelia and Mr Wombat
- Some of the girls from Twisters, the gymnastical club Zoe and I go to.

**4** Names of people we would rather **not** join our flash mob (with reasons for and against):

- Precious Perfect Princess Peach Parker
- And also her princesses-in-waiting, Prinny and Jade

## Reasons For

1. They are all really good (especially Peach) at doing dancing and gymnastical stuff.

2. That's it. There is NO reason number 2.

## Reasons Against

1. Because Princess Peach ALWAYS has to be the best at everything.

2. And get her own way.

3. And also boss everyone else around.

4. And she would tell her princesses-in-waiting to boss everyone around as well.

We had **HEAPS** more points we could have added to the Reasons Against list but we didn't get a chance to write any of them down because . . .

**Da Da Da...DUMMMMM.**

Someone was heading straight, directly, unswervingly (and also undeviatingly*) towards us.

* Undeviatingly means exactly the same thing as straight, directly and unswervingly. Which means not swerving or moving out of the straight line you are travelling in from Point A to Point B.

Even if you are being chased by an angry armadillo.

And guess who it was?

If you said **Princess Peach** you are 100 per cent correct!

Here's what we all said.

**Princess Peach** (brightly): Hi, girls!
**Me, Zoe and Ammy** (unbrightly): Hello.
**Princess Peach:** So, I hear you're all doing a flash mob. For Mother's Day.

(How does she even know this? We haven't said **ANYTHING to ANYONE** about it yet. Not even Cordelia and Mr Wombat. It's just like the other night when Olivia obviously knew what I think about her time machine. **SPOOOOKY!**

**Me, Zoe and Ammy** (shocked): 😮😮😮

**Princess Peach** (brightlier): We totes LOVE doing flash mobs, don't we, Prinny and Jade.

**Prinny and Jade**: Totes.

**Princess Peach** (even more brightly): And doing one for Mother's Day is such a clever idea.

**Prinny and Jade** (nodding): The best.

**Princess Peach**: So when do we start rehearsing for it?

**Zoe and Ammy** (puzzled): Ummmm . . .

**Me** (even more puzzled): We . . . er . . . we haven't actually decided yet.

**Princess Peach** (smilingly): That's OK! Just let me know when you do. I've done HEAPS of flash mobs so I already know some REALLY cool moves. It's going to be SO fun!

And then she and Prinny and Jade pranced away to the other side of the playground, tossing their hair like show ponies.

Zoe and Ammy and I stared at each other.

**WARNING:**

**SHOCK ALERT!**

SO shocked, we decided to have a quick Emergency Meeting about it, right there on our special bench. (Even though we didn't have any snacks.)

This time, we only had ONE IMPORTERANT THING we needed to discuss:

# SHOULD WE LET PEACH JOIN OUR FLASH MOB?

Zoe said no, because she would ruin everything **ruinously** just like she always does.

But then Ammy reminded us that Peach was a really good dancerer and also gymnast. And that she'd done flash mobs before, so would be able to give us some good tips about what moves and steps to do*.

* Especially as we didn't know any yet.

And then I said she was probably just fibbing about that—like the time she told us her aunty from Timbuktooty is a world famorous synchronised swimming star (and also coach). Or that she had three sweet little baby goats living in her back shed.

And then Ammy reminded us that Mother's Day was coming up really, really, REALLY fast, so we'd better make up our minds soon.

So we made a **SNAP** decision.

We'd give Peach (and also her friends) **ONE** chance only. And if she got too **bossy** or **pushy** or **annoying** we would ask her and her princesses-in-waiting to leave imMEDiately. And also straightaway.

Then we all did our **special handshake** to show our EM was officially over and skipped off to the canteen to get some fruit tingles.

Love,

Ella

## Tuesday night, in bed

Dearest Diary,

We had our very first **Mother's Day Flash Mob** (MDFM) meeting today!

First we asked Ms Weiss if it was OK to have it at school. And she said **YES!** ☺

Then we passed notes about it to the OIs (Official Invitees) in our class.

This is what the notes looked like.

Dear.............. Name of Oi goes **HERE**

You have been **Officially** invited to

Join the **MOTHER'S DAY**

**FLASH MOB!**

Please meet the **FMC** (FLASH MOB COMMITTEE)
at the back of the BasketBall courts
(under the **BIG** pine trees) at 1:15.

**WARNING: DO NOT BE LATE!!!**

Signed: Ella Ammy Zoe

We also gave some notes to Carly from Twisters at recess time, to pass on to our other friends in her class. With ~~STRICK~~ ~~STRICKT~~ STRICT INSTRUCTIONS to be ON TIME.

Then, at exactly 1.14, Zoe and Ammy and I took up our ~~posizions~~ positions under the pine trees at the back of the basketball courts.

We waited

and waited

and waited

until—finally—everyone we invited turned up!

Here's what they said:

So then Zoe and Ammy and I explained to everyone:

a) what a flash mob was (with actions), and

b) how we were going to do one in the park for Mother's Day, as a lovely surprise for our mums, and

c) how we wanted them all to join in so it would be SUPER SPECTACULAR.

And guess what? Princess Peach and her two princesses-in-waiting didn't try to interrupt. Or boss us around. Or even show everyone a better way to do a move.

Not. Even. Once.

They just stood there sweetly, listening politely as we explained everything.

All our friends thought doing a Mother's Day Flash Mob was a **BRILLIANT** idea. And also **excellent**. And **amazing**. And **fantabulously fabulous!**

Some of them even made up a few flash mob moves themselves, right there on the spot.

And the gymnastical girls from Twisters said if we were doing our flash mob in the park, we could try performing some of our moves on the playground equipment.

Like the monkey bars

or the swings

or even the giganterous slide!

And then Carly from Twisters said, 'What if you've got two mums?'

'Same,' said Ammy. 'Which one do I invite? Because sometimes I live with Mum and sometimes with Dad and my step-mum, Grace.'

OOPS. I'd forgotten all about Ammy's two mums.

Zoe and I gave each other worried looks, mainly because we weren't sure how to answer the question. What if you only asked one of your mums to come to the park, and then the other one found out and was really sad? ☹

And then Peach asked Carly and Ammy a question.

And then Poppy said, 'What if you haven't even got a mum? Can you still be in it?'

Double OOPS! I'd forgotten that Poppy lived alone with her dad.

Peach said maybe Poppy could bring her nanna or aunty or dad instead. Like other kids at our school do when we have Mother's Day special events.

And Poppy gave her a **big smile** and said that's what she always did too. And this time she was going to bring along her mum's sister, Aunty Steph.

**Zow-ie.** Peach was being **REALLY** helpful. And also super nice. She wasn't even looking bored or giving sharkerous smiles, like she usually does. What was going on?

Anyway, after that we tried out a few different moves until the bell went and we all went back to class.

It was **funnerous fun**, Diary! I can't wait until tomorrow when we have our next meeting.

Yours 4 ever and ever,

Ella

XXX

## Wednesday, after dinner

Dear Diary,

We had another MDFM meeting at lunchtime today.

This time, after trying out some more moves, we had a **big chat** about how the music would work.

I really wanted to have some **drummers** playing their **African drums**, like the ones I saw at the shopping centre the other day.

~~Unforch~~ Unfortunately, I don't know any drummers who play African drums. The only drummer I know is my second cousin Wesley who plays in a **heavy metal band***.

* A heavy metal band is a band that plays **extremely loud** and **noiserous** music with thumping drums and squealing guitars that my dad says give him a headache. It is NOT a band made out of heavy metals like gold or lead.

So then Cordelia said maybe we could ask Fiona McTavish (who is also in our class) to play some lovely music on her bagpipes.

But then Zoe helpfully pointed out that we wouldn't ~~acksh~~ actually be dancing any Scottish reels in our flash mob, so bagpipes might not be the right sound for us.

So we all sat there for a moment having a quiet think about music and musical instruments until . . .

TA DAA!

. . . something suddenly flashed into my brain . . .

. . . at **EXACTLY** the same time something flashed into Peach's.

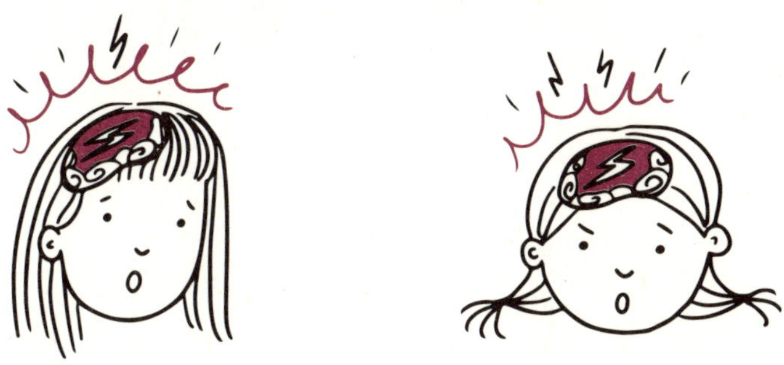

We looked at each other with shiny eyes. As shiny as the shiny bits on a trumpet. And also a tuba. And a French horn. And then this happened.

And then we both laughed like a pair of **laughing hyenas**. Just like we used to do when we were little girls in Grade 3 before the **BIG INCIDENT** happened.

And guess what the something that flashed into our brains was?

You probably never will even if you had a pazillion guesses every year for a bazillion years, so I'll just tell you.

## Cassi Valentine!

Cassi Valentine is my most **favouritist singer of all time**. And also Zoe's. And Ammy's. And Poppy's and Daisy's and Chloe's and Georgia's. In fact, she is the favourite singer of all the girls in my class. And probably our **whole entire school!**

Her music would be **PERFECT** for our flash mob to do our moves to.

So anyway, Peach and I told all our friends about what we'd been thinking.

And guess what they said?

If you think they said, 'Eww, no thanks', you are **WRONG, WRONG, WRONG!**

They said things like **aMAZing** and **fanTABulous** and **AWEsome** and **YES PLEASE!**

So then we all had another big think about which Cassi Valentine song we should choose for our MDFM.

But we couldn't think of any that had the right words in them. Not even one. ☹☹☹

And then the weirdest thing in the history of weird things happened. SO weird I think I might even have imagined it.

Peach leaned in really, really close to me and whispered something in my ear. Like this.

And this is what she said to me:

'You're really, really good at writing poems and song lyrics, Ella. Why don't YOU write the words to the song we sing for the flash mob?'

And then she also told me her other aunty* could come to her place one day to record my song. And we could play it in the park through **special speakers** while we were doing the flash mob.

* Not the one from Timbuktooty who was a synchronised swimming star and coach. This one is a famous music producer with her own recording studio.

I was **SHOCKED**. But also a teeny tiny bit confused (and also **mystified, baffled**

and **befuddled**). Why was Peach being so nice to me? Were we going to become BFFs again???

Yours in puzzlement,

Ella

XOXO

## Thursday, after school

Dear Diary,

We worked on some really **importerant stuff** at our MDFM today.

Like who was going to be the single person right at the start.

And who was going to join them next, and then next after that, and in what order.

And where we would all be in the park while we were waiting for our bit to start.

And where we would do the actual flash mob dance, once everyone was together.

It was fun! Like doing a **giganterous maths problem**. Cordelia helped us figure it all out, because she's really good at all that kind of stuff.

Meanwhile, Peach got everyone practising all the different moves.

We're going to do some really cool things, like

the Stretch and Point

and the Step and Stomp

and the Wiggle and Giggle

and the Rumble Bumble

and the strike
a pose.

Everything's coming together **really** well!

Love,
Ella

## Friday night, in bed

Dear Diary,

I am super super angry (and also furiously fuming) to the power of a patrillion!

Ammy and I and also Priya (who is extremely good at doing costuming stuff) were supposed to be going to Zoe's place after school today so we could have a **Mother's Day Flash Mob Costume Emergency Meeting** (MDFMCEM). I'd even started jotting down a few design ideas for it in my **special Ideas Jotter.**

And guess what happened?

Olivia told Mum that she needed a haircut really really badly. SO badly that if she didn't get one STRAIGHTAWAY IMMEDIATELY she was going to walk around the house crashing into everything because her fringe was too long to see through.

And guess what happened next? You never will so I'll just tell you.

Mum told Olivia she thought that her getting a haircut was an excellent idea.

And that Max and I looked like we needed one too. And that she'd been wanting to get her OWN haircut for ages.

And then she told Olivia and me to hurry up and get changed out of our school uniforms so we could all have a nice trip to Haircuts'R'US at the big shopping centre.

And she wouldn't change her mind, even when I reminded her that I was supposed to be going to Zoe's place to work on a project together*.

* Luckily, she didn't ask me about the project . . . what if I had to tell her **THE REAL REASON?** That would **TOTALLY** spoil our MDFM surprise. ☹

So then I had to quickly call Zoe and tell her that she and Ammy and Priya would have to have the meeting without me.

It was **SO NOT FAIR**, Diary! I was really looking forward to showing them my ideas.

Why are little sisters always SO annoying?

E

X

### About ten minutes later . . .

Oooooo. I forgot to tell you. While we were

at the big shopping centre I saw some really sweet **little T-shirts** in the window of Bella Tees.

And guess what they had on the front of them?

T-shirts like that would make **PERFECT** costumes for our MDFM.

I can't wait to tell the committee about it tomorrow!

Goodnight.

Sleep tight.

Don't let the

Love Hearts bite!

Yours 4 ever,

Ella

XOXOX

## Saturday night, before dinner

Dear Diary,

So much aMAZing stuff happened today I'm not sure what to tell you first.

So I'll start at the beginning. ☺

I was just admiring my new haircut in the mirror when Olivia banged on my door and said there was a **phone call** for me. And could I hurry up please because she was busy working on her time machine. (Ha! ☺)

And guess who was on the phone?

**HINT:** It rhymes with this.

If you said **Zoe** you are correct!

Zoe said she and Ammy and Priya didn't end up having our MDFMCEM yesterday because they didn't think it was fair to have it without me being there. Seeing as how the flash mob was my idea and everything.

AWWWWWWWW. That is **SOOOO** sweet. ☺☺☺

Anyway, she also asked if I would be available to have it this morning instead.

At Ammy's house this time.

And I was. **So we did!**

And I told them all about my idea to have everyone wearing T-shirts with **big love hearts** stuck on the front of them.

And Ammy said she knew a place through her mum's work where we could get ♥heart stickers♥ from.

And Zoe said we wouldn't even need to buy new T-shirts. Everyone could just stick their heart onto an old T-shirt or plain top they already had.

And then Priya had an even betterer idea! We could all start off wearing jackets or cardigans. And then when we got to a certain part of the song, we could RRRIPPPP! them off so our mums could see the love hearts on the T-shirts underneath!

YES! It was a **fantabulous** idea!

Have to stop writing now, Diary. Dad just

called out to let me know dinner is ready. I'll come back later, I promise! The next part is going to be SUPER AMAZING!

E.

**After dinner . . .**

I'm back. Mum made stir-fried noodles. YUM! She really is the BESTEST mum in the whole wild world. (She just doesn't know it yet. ☺)

So anyway, after lunch at Ammy's place, we all went on a TOP SECRET MISSION to the park to meet up with the other flash mobbers, so we could work out all the best places to do our dance.

THIS SPOT was Perfect FOR US!

Carly and Marisa and Priya even busted a few moves* on the monkey bars!

* Marisa told me saying things like 'bust a move' is the way people who do a special kind of dancing (like breakdancing**) speak.

** Breakdancing does **NOT** mean you ~~acksh~~ actually break any body parts while you are dancing, like your leg or arm or ankle parts. (That would just be WEIRD.) It is a **super energetic** type of dance, with lots of kicks and spins. Like these:

And guess who we saw while we were at the park?

The **circus kids!** Their names are Esther and Lottie and Willem. They came over to watch the Twisters girls practising some moves on the monkey bars. Lottie even joined in!

And guess what else? They ♥ our idea about doing a Mother's Day Flash Mob. So they're going to come too.

Esther and Willem are even going to do some **tightrope walking** while we're all dancing and busting moves!

It's going to be bigger than the biggest thing in the history of BIG THINGS! ☺

CYA later,
Ell Pell

## Sunday night, in bed

Dear Diary,

Nanna Kate asked Olivia and Max and me

to help weed her special garden space at the Community Gardens today, so we couldn't do any rehearsing or have any meetings for the You Know What. ☹

And now I'm having some Quiet Time in my room, so I can work on my MDFM song.

There are only seven more sleeps until Mother's Day. And I need to have it finished in time for Peach's Aunty Suzy to record it this week.

Writing songs is **HARD WORK**, Diary.

Especially when they have to be as special as this one.

Wish me luck!

E

XX

## Monday night, after dinner

Dear Diary-Doo,

We did some **special super-secret** rehearsing at school today.

And guess what we're going to do right at the end?

Instead of running off all over the park again, we're going to make a big **LOVE HEART** that goes all around our mothers and others!

It's going to look like this. ☺

I can't wait until Sunday to see Mum's face!

Ella xoxo

## Tuesday, before dinner

Dear Diary,

Ammy brought a big pile of red heart stickers to school today. She had to tell her mum what they were going to be used for*, but she cleverly managed to do that **AND** keep our plan a surprise. Hehehe.

* A **super secret surprise project** she was doing with me and Zoe.

We handed them out to all the flash mobbers at our lunchtime rehearsal so they could stick them onto their

T-shirts, ready for the Big Reveal!

I stuck mine on as soon as I got home from school. ~~Unforch~~ Unfortunately, Olivia barged into my room (without being invited) while I was checking what it looked like in the mirror.

No way! I bet she's been **SPYING** on me again.

She'd better not try to muck up our plans.

Still working on my song . . .

~~Dearest **MUM**, I Love **YOU**~~
~~You're my **STAR** when I feel **BLUE**~~

Ella x

## Wednesday night, in bed, very very late . . .

Still working on my song . . .

E

## Thursday, after dinner

Dearest **Darlingest** Diary,

I finally finished my song last night!

**PHEW!**

That's because Peach invited me to go to her place after school today so her Aunty Suzy (the **famorous record-producer** one) could record me singing it.

Well, ~~acksh~~ actually, that should say US singing it, rather than just 'me'. That's because Peach asked me **really really nicely** if she could sing my song on the recording as well.

SO nicely that I couldn't really say no. (Especially as it was her aunty doing the recordering part.)

It's going to sound **aMAZing** on the day!

Yours 4 Ever,

Ella

XX

## Friday night, after dinner

Dear Diary,

We had our **final, last ever rehearsal** for the dance section of our MDFM at school today. And the flash mobbers were **ON FIRE!** We didn't even make any mistakes!

The **Twisters girls** also did a few sneakerous moves on the playground equipment to make sure their part was working well.

Esther and Lottie and Willem are going to meet us at the park tomorrow, so we can run through some of the **moves** with them before Sunday.

Oh, and the **most importerant** thing. I asked Mum if she would like to come for a lovely walk to the park on Sunday with me and Bob (leaving out the special secret surprise part of course☺).

And guess what she said????

Yes!

**PHEW**.

OK, going to sleep now, Diary. I need to make sure I have **MAXIMUM ENERGY** for our BIG DAY!

But first I'm going to have one last listen to the song I wrote for Mum.

I can't wait to see her face when she sees what we've organerised for her special day!

E x

## Saturday night

Dear Diary,

I am in **desperating despair!** We couldn't go to meet the circus kids at the park today because there was a **giganterous thunderstorm**. And then it rained **ALL DAY LONG WITHOUT STOPPING.**

What if they muck up all their parts?

But more importerantly, what if it rains again tomorrow?!!!

E

## Sunday night

Dear Diary,

When I woke up this morning the sun was streaming streamerously through my window.

It felt like a pazillion cute puppies had just given me a bazillion cuddly licks and hugs. Today was going to be SO MUCH FUN!

I ran into the kitchen where Mum was sitting at the table eating a special Mother's Day (MD for short) breakfast made by Max.

I was just opening my mouth to remind Mum about our lovely MD walk to the park this afternoon when . . . something **horrendously horrifying** happened. So horrendously horrifyingly I wanted to run back to my room and hide in there **FOREVER!**

Olivia asked Mum if she wanted to go to the shopping centre after lunch as she had a **special surprise** planned for her.

**NOOOOOOOOoo!**

What if Mum said yes? All my plans for a super-special Mother's Day surprise would be **RUINED!**

~~Forch~~ Fortunately, she didn't.

She said this instead:

**Mum** (kindly): That sounds lovely, Possum!
**Olivia** (cunningly): ☺
**Mum** (explainingly): But I've already arranged to go to the park with your sister. You should come too. And Max.
**Olivia** (upsettedly): But I CAN'T! I . . . ummm . . . I . . .
**Mum** (firmly): That's settled then. It's going to be fun!
**Olivia**: ☹☹☹

**PHEW** to the power of a patrillion and six!

Why do little sisters have to be **SO**

annoying all the time??? Olivia is probably just upset that she didn't think of doing a flash mob first. I bet there wasn't even a real surprise.

Anyway, as soon as we'd finished lunch I changed into my MDFM T-shirt, popped my jacket over the top, and set off with Mum and Bob and Olivia to the park.

It was **SO EXCITERATING**, Diary! I could see all the other flash mobbers (including the circus kids) hanging out in different parts of the park with their mothers or others. And they were all being **EXTRA EXTRA** careful to pretend not to notice that any of their friends were there. ☺

And then Carly stood in the middle of the grassy lawn bit, and looked meaningfully at her watch.

And a few seconds later, Poppy joined her.

Then all the other dancing flash mobbers came **rushing over** from every single corner of the park, and formed three lines.

Peach's Aunty Suzy **hit the button** on the boom box . . . and we started **dancing** to my song!

Like this:

Our mothers and others went crazy!

Especially when the Twisters girls moved over to the monkey bars and swings. And then the **circus kids** joined in beside them with their circus tricks!

And then . . . **POUFF!** My song finished. And we all stopped dancing and gymnasticking and circus tricking and formed our big love heart, winding winderously all the way around our lovely mothers and others.

It felt **aMAZing** And **EXcellent** And **fanTABulously fabulous**

Our mothers and others stood in **stunned silence** for a few nanoseconds. Then they all rushed over to give us a hug.

And guess what happened after that?

Zoe and Ammy and I (and our mums) were standing right next to Peach and her mum. And we heard them saying **THIS** to each other:

Then she show-ponied back to her friends.

But **I'm** the one who wrote the song! What if Peach tells everyone she did? And they believe her?

**NOOOOOOOO!**

Zoe and Ammy and I looked at each other, shocked.

And then Zoe put her arm around me and I said Peach had probably just been acting all **nicey-nicey** so I'd let her be in the flash mob and take ALL the credit for writing **MY** song. ☹

But then Ammy said that she and Zoe would tell their mums (and also mine) who **really** wrote the song. And Zoe said, 'As long as our mums know who really wrote it, that's what matters most, right?'

I don't need Peach to be my **BFF**. I already have **HEAPS** of real ones.

Like these two. ☺☺☺

Love and hugs,

Ella

XOXOXO

## PS About five minutes later . . .

OOPS! I forgot to tell you the most **importerant** part!

On the way home from the park, Mum (and also Zoe's and Ammy's mums) couldn't stop talking about our flash mob.

And then when we got home, Mum told Dad how aMAZing it was all over again! And how proud she was of me for thinking it all up—especially my **BEAUTIFUL** song. And then Dad said, 'Oh wow! I wonder if I'll get a gift as amazing as that for Father's Day?'

And guess what Olivia said? You never will, so I'll just tell you.

And then she turned to me and said, in her most annoying voice, 'And by the way, **YOU'RE** not doing Father's Day this year. **MATILDA AND I** are.'

HEHEHE. I wonder what Olivia is planning. Sometimes her ideas are almost as **aMAZing** as mine!

Maybe that's why I ♥ her. ☺☺☺

**PPS Five seconds later . . .**

But don't EVER let her find out I wrote that, OK? ☺

# Ella's Song

Hey, Mum—I love you
For all the wonderful things you do
Yay, Mum—you're the best
Bazillions better than all the rest!
Flipping pancakes
Jumping puddles
Reading stories
Giving cuddles
Every day and every night
Working hard to make things right!
Solving problems
Offering hugs
Planning parties
Catching slugs! (Ewww.)
Hey, Mum—I love you
For all the fabulous things you do
Yay, Mum—you're the best
Pazillions more than all the rest!

♥ U Mum 4 EVER!!!

# ELLA Diaries

Read more of Ella's brilliant diary in

- Double Dare You
- Ballet Backflip
- I ♥ Pets
- Dreams come true
- Christmas Chaos
- Pony School Showdown
- Friends Forever
- Worst Camp Ever
- Operation Merry Christmas
- Friendship S.O.S
- Going Green
- Total TV Drama
- Goal Power
- Diary Disaster
- The Super Secret Club
- Gym Squad Tumble
- Time to Shine
- Wildlife Rescue!
- Passion for Fashion
- Christmas Crackers
- Diva Drama
- Camp Gold Rush
- Spooky Surprise
- Dolphin Dreaming
- Museum Mayhem
- Fundraising Frenzy

and look out for more coming soon!